I0470635

The 7 Deadly Sins of Advertising
and
How to Avoid Them

Small Business Marketing

By Glyn Williams

http://marketingformugs.com

Join the mailing list at
marketingformugs.com
for more great tips on marketing your
business

You'll also get to see a video relating to this
book

Table of Contents

Introduction

It's a sad fact that only 18% of advertising efforts on radio and TV actually produce a positive return on investment. In newspapers the retention rate of an advert is around 22%. That means that ON AVERAGE 78 people out of 100 looking at a newspaper ad don't even remember it let alone actually buy the product.

This book aims to make sure that the money that YOU spend is spent wisely and gets you above those figures. If you are in business and using advertising for that business then I'm confident that this small book will help you to use that advertising with greater effect.

It's important to point out that the things that I'm going to share with you in this book are from the real world. I really get annoyed with authors of books on marketing that have never sold so much as a bag of beans and yet profess to know everything there is to know about sales, marketing and how to advertise.

For 25 years I've been involved in business, many of which have been my own. I've sold advertising, music, clothing, energy, windows, doors, discos, records, software, hardware, books, events, timber, sponsorships, industrial chemicals, pesticides, electronic goods, cleaning services, home improvements, publications and much more that I have probably forgotten about.

I don't tell you this to impress you but to impress upon you that you're going to discover inside these pages tools and techniques that actually work in the real world. I've done this for a living and I've been where you are now. The product or service may be different but sales are sales no matter what you have to peddle.

In advertising terms I ran the commercial department of a small radio station for four of those 25 years and ran my own station for another three years too. I've written thousands of radio commercials have advertised my own businesses in newspapers and magazines and have collected much research over the years. Commercials I have written for clients have made over £2million in business.

A full 'About The Author' section resides near the end of the book if you want to learn more.

What I'm trying to get across here is that I'm not one of those myriad of people that write a book having had no real experience. They are the armchair experts sat in front of the TV watching the real experts and being able to explain what's happening. Put them in the same arena though and they don't have a clue what to do.

In my time as a marketing consultant I have found that a large number of people operating small businesses are very good at what they do and the services that they provide. However, they are not so good at marketing with a view to increasing the sales of those products and services.

When these well intentioned business owners take out their advertising they often make the "big mistakes", and there are several of them. In fact, I'm describing them as The "Seven Deadly Sins of Advertising."

This book describes what each of the seven deadly sins of advertising actually are and I will also show you how to avoid making them with a simple systemic process that gets you ready to generate sales for your business.

The process is not difficult. Many marketing people like to wrap advertising creation in what amounts to gobbledygook; but in practice the method used to design and create advertising messages are pretty simple. Simple enough that anyone can do it, including you!

The book is designed in two parts. During the first part we identify the 7 deadly sins and learn what those mistakes are and more importantly how they are responsible for the failing of hundreds of thousands of advertisements. Once you know what they are then you can avoid them.

The second part of the book gives you a system in which most of the deadly sins are avoided. The system gets you into the mind of your target prospect and helps you to see things from their viewpoint.

The system also covers your branding and how to get that right so it generates business time and time again

It's an experiential book so grab yourself a notepad and get ready to use it. After all knowledge may indeed be power but the application of that knowledge will be what makes this successful for you.

Each chapter in the book has action points for you to follow.

Enjoy!

The Seven Deadly Sins of Advertising

I've got to tell you up front that there are actually eight deadly sins, but I wanted a catchier headline! The eight deadly sins just didn't cut it.

Maybe I misled you a little from the title of the book but at least I'm over delivering!

The rules here that we are going to talk about applies to Posters, to Flyers, to Radio, to Television, to Newspapers, Garden Signs, calendars, banners trailing behind an aeroplane, to absolutely anything that you decide to use to advertise your business. So, let's get down to it:

Do you ever find yourself saying this, "Sometimes it fees that no matter what you do your advertising just doesn't work." Is it the message? Is it the media that you're using? Or is it just that business is no good?

The chances are that you are making several of the mistakes we are about to go through. If everyone knows you buy no-one buys then you have no compelling reason for them to do so but your branding is ok. If you advertise everywhere but no-one really knows you then there's a problem with your branding.

As you stand at the moment you don't know what you don't know.

Allow me to introduce you to the first sin ....

Deadly Sin No 1

Deadly Sin No 1: 'Advertising Your Business'

Your prospect, the person that you're trying to get to buy from you, does not care about your business. They don't care at all. They only care about what your business can do for them.

Think about that. The fact that you've "been established 20 years", or "have got seven branches", or you "give service with a smile," or whatever you put there that is about you, has no bearing whatsoever on their decision to purchase from you.

The things that you think are important are not. You think that people want to buy from a solid company that will be here next year if they have a problem. You think that they will buy if they like you; you think they will buy if they know you have seven branches or if you treat your staff well.

Here's glaring truth number one for you. **No-one gives a toss about your business but you.**

Now think about how many times do you tell people how brilliant your business is in your advertising? You put down "established x number of years," "we do this," "we do that', "we, we, we, our this, our that."

Here are a few examples of what the self centred business advertiser puts in their message:

- **Established XX years**
- **Service with a smile**
- **We go the extra mile**
- **Serving the local community**
- **For all your widget needs**
- **An xxx for all occasions**
- **We care about your business**

- **We are the local specialist**
- **For a friendly and reliable service**
- **We are unique**
- **Our Professional home design service**
- **Everyone recommends us**

You are probably sceptical about this, many people are. I had a very spirited debate with a carpet outlet once that said telling people how long they've been in business was of major importance. I then asked him "tell me the last time you purchased something for the sole reason that the company had been in business for 10 years" you know the answer.

Think why you buy things yourself. Next time you are looking to buy something ask yourself why am I buying from here? And why am I buying now? That's how your customers think.

Most people can work out what your basic services are from your business name. If you can't then you've got a problem to start with because your business name should really say what you do.

The message in this deadly sin is that many advertising messages are all *me, me, me,* when they should really be *you, you, you*.

Next time you're writing advertising copy count the number of "we," "our" and "my," in your advertising message, and then the number of "you" mentions like "you," and "yours," That will tell you a story.

The correct ratio by the way is about 4:1, believe it or not. There should be around 4 *you's* to one *me*.

Action: get a local newspaper and look at the advertisements in there. Highlight the ones that are all Me, Me, Me and then ask yourself "would I buy that?"

Then look at the advertisements that you may be interested in - what do they do? Chances are they look at a problem that you have to solve and then offer a solution.

That's the formula you must get used to using.

Deadly Sin No 2

Deadly Sin No 2: Too Much Content

Just before I dig into this one please allow me to cover the difference between an advertisement and a campaign. An advertisement is a single piece of copy or design and a campaign is a series of advertisements with a single theme.

For the most part this book will deal with single advertisements rather than campaigns.

Here is a golden rule. It's what I call the "Rule of one."

You should aim for, in each advertising message: **One product or service, to One target prospect, for One reason.**

An advertisement should have one single product or service not ten. If you have more than one product then you need more than one campaign.

I've lost count of the number of times that people have come to me, and said "We want to advertise Glyn, what advice can you give us?" And I'll say, "Well what do you want to do? What do you want to advertise?" And they'll say something like, "Oh, we've got shoes on sale, we've got hats on sale, and we've also got a cafe now that does coffee and things; like cakes and scones. Next week we've got an event on in the night time where we're having a fancy dress party."

It's too many products. **One product, to One target, for One reason.** That is the golden rule. You will hear it several times in this book

Another example of this is solicitors and lawyers, - I'm not picking on you guys if that's what you do, but solicitors and lawyers do family law, conveyancing, wills, criminal law, landlord legal's etc etc. There are a lot of areas that they cover. What they tend to do in their advertising is try and cover all of those products in one message.

This is a scatter gun approach where as we want to be the sniper!

What actually happens is you end up leaving the person that's listening or reading your advertisement confused; switching off; thinking that 'this is nothing to do with me'. Whereas concentrating on one area gives you much better response. So don't be too general in an advertising message. Each product or service should have its own campaign.

Later in the book you will learn how to choose this product.

Action: I want you to listen to a radio commercial this time. In particular to a local station with a local business advertising. Listen for the message. Notice if you get the message or if you get several of them. Notice the different way you feel about commercials with multiple messages.

Do the same thing with a newspaper. Notice how the strongest advertisements are those with a single message that hits hard.

Deadly Sin No 3

Deadly Sin No 3: Choosing The Medium First

Most advertising sales happen because a slick advertising rep gets in touch with you in some way and convinces you that their medium is the best.

"We've got loads of people reading our newspaper; we've got loads of people listening to our radio station" "we can distribute to thousands" and they convince you that their target is what you need.

But choosing the medium to advertise with is not the first step; it's actually the last one.

The first steps are to define your target; then hone your message; and finally find out where to advertise. If you allow yourself to be sold then that salesman has all of the power. They define how you will communicate with their audience. They convince you that it's right for you.

The process we will go through in part two of this book will shift the power back to you. You will know your target, you will know your message and if the slick sales rep doesn't have your target then they are of no use to you. Even if they gave it to you for free!

A good fisherman will go where the fish are biting, and that's what you have to do. But until you know the kind of fish that you're looking for; you don't know which river to fish in.

Action: If you are considering an offer from an advertising rep right now, just hold off until you've completed this book. By the end you will know the audience you need and you can ask the rep to tell you their demographic. Any rep worth a bean will have that information and you will be able to see if there is a match.

Deadly Sin No 4

Deadly Sin No 4: Inconsistent Branding

There are two types of advertising **"Branding"** and **"Response."**

The best kind of advertising uses both.

Branding does sell your business but it takes time to kick in. I've had a few discussions on social media of late with people regarding branding, some believe that branding is pointless for small businesses and they shouldn't even bother doing it because they haven't got the budget. That is total bollocks.

Every business needs a brand. Branding does sell but branding is something that sells over time. Does that mean you should forget about it? Of course not!

Your brand is something that will bring your name to mind the next time someone is looking for your product or service. This is because they've seen your brand over and over and over again, in your response advertising.

Branding in simple terms are graphics that support the company ethos, a consistent strapline that says what your business does or believes in, and a feel for how you want your business to be perceived.

Beware though; the branding must match the business. If your branding says that you target a high end market, like stately homes, or big corporate companies, then it's not going to fit in if your office or your place of business is the back of a garage. Don't try and build yourself up to something that you're not. Or indeed, put yourself down to something that you're above.

Make sure that your brand is truly consistent with your business and that your brand is used in every single piece of advertising you create. You create a brand and then you leverage it. Where else can you put it?

Once you have your brand (and we will do this later) you must be consistent. Use the same brand every time you advertise. I once went to one company that had seventeen straplines! How on earth can you embed this into your prospect's mind when you're constantly changing it?

We will cover more on branding and how to get your branding right later in the book. There are also some articles on our blog over at Marketing For Mugs, In particular this one and this one

Right now as I write this book there is a series of TV commercials for Virgin Media. They sell TV, Broadband and telephony services in the UK. Every commercial is different but every commercial is the same. At the end of every commercial whoever the 'star' presenter is they draw the logo on screen and wipe their finger across the bottom as the web address appears. Take note of this - If huge corporations can do this so can you.

Action: take a look at various advertisements over several weeks. Look for those who use different branding every time and how there is an inconsistency to their advertisements. Then look at the big national advertisers. The same every time.

Deadly Sin No 5

Deadly Sin No 5: Missing Call To Action

Your advertising has a reason. You want someone to do something as a result of reading or hearing it. Your advertising must have a call to action and the prospect must know what you want them to do.

The only way they will know what you want them to do is if you tell them. Even if it's "call now on 12345" or "book your appointment now" or "click calltoaction.com", you have to tell them what to do.

If you don't then they won't know to do it and believe it or not, they genuinely will not do it unless you ask for it.

Also, with the use of the call to action you should inject some scarcity for your offerings; make it a 'buy now' kind of thing, "Visit our showroom before they're all gone. There are only 20 left." Direct salesmen are very good at this. (More later)

It's really simple to find your call to action. What do you want them to do? Once you've worked out *specifically* what you want them to do then make sure you tell them.

Action: scan the newspapers and listen to the radio and find some advertisements without a call to action. More importantly notice the ones that have.

Deadly Sin No 6

Deadly Sin No 6: No Compelling Reason to Buy

What is the point of advertising? Answer that to yourself in your head right now. Why do you advertise?

If your answer is anything else but 'to make sales' then you're mistaken.

'Awareness' is an answer I often get to that question, "Oh it's for awareness of my business.". Now ask why do you want awareness? Why? Why do you want people to be aware? So they come and buy from you or use your service.

Even if your service is free, for example in public services, you still want them to make the conscious decision to buy from you; **it's all about sales.** Never forget that!

So, "no compelling reason to buy" may be deadly sin number six on my list, but it is the number one reason for advertising failing to produce a result.

If you don't give your prospects a compelling reason to buy then guess what, they won't. This is why many small businesses spend thousands and thousands on advertising and generate zip, *nada*, nothing form it; zero sales.

If you've ever said, "Everyone knows about my business but no one buys," this is the most likely reason why that happens. You may have had a great advertisement and good branding which is why everyone knows; but without that compelling reason they simply will not buy.

A compelling reason to buy is some kind of offer. Now that doesn't have to be a discount, everybody thinks "what compelling offer can I give", and they often come up with, "Oh I'll do 20% off, 30% off, I'll do it half price."

Smart business people realise it's not all about cost. It could be a free item to go with the original purchase. It could be a free entry into a prize draw for something substantial, or it could be something totally unrelated to the product. Let your imagination run wild here.

Important words: **an offer should make you money, not cost you money**. A good offer will do that. You'll make more money than you would without the offer, and having an offer with just a discount doesn't do that unless you sell shedloads of product because of that discount. These days the discount offer is actually very weak.

Later we will talk about your compelling offer and how to put one together including how to add a scarcity value to make your prospects not just want to buy, but want to buy NOW

Action: Guess what? Yep I want you to look at commercials and advertisements again and identify those with compelling reasons. Take notes of any ideas that you think you could use in your own business.

Deadly Sin No 7

Deadly Sin No 7: The Same Message to Different Targets

It's important that your advertising is targeted. Very important!

Now I know you are thinking 'of course' you may think that targeting is just making sure that the people you market to actually need your product. After all you wouldn't advertise wheelchairs in an athletic magazine would you. (Aside from Paralympics ones perhaps!)

Targeting has to be much more specific than just choosing a market that wants your product.

Using the same message to a man who wants your product or services for one reason, will not apply to a women that wants it for something totally different. You must get very specific on who you want to target, and why they will buy from you. One message will not resonate with all of the people that use your product. This is how the concept of a *campaign* is born.

Campaign: a collection of advertisements for the same product to different targets

I'm going to give you an example then: *the drill bit.* I like using this example; I've done a few talks here and there, and this is one that I use quite regularly.

If you're a hardware store, and someone buys an 8mm drill bit from you, what do they really want? That's a question that I'm asking you, what do they really want if they're buying an 8mm drill bit?

Now I'll give you a tip because I know the first thing that came into your head was "they want an 8mm hole" and that's not true either. What the customer probably wants is a shelf, and on that shelf he might want to display his medals to make him feel good. He might not even want a shelf; he might want to hang a picture up or just to fix a chair that's broken.

There are a million reasons for wanting an 8mm drill bit. And, none of the underlying reasons are to do with the actual drill bit. Knowing what people want to do with your product is imperative. If you don't know why people buy then start asking them. That's where you will really find your target markets.

It's imperative that you know the reasons that people buy what you sell and what they do with it. It's also imperative to know why they chose to buy it from YOU rather than from your competition.

Action: start doing some research as to why people buy the things you want to promote. You won't find a better source of answers to this question that people that have already bought and paid for it. That's right, your customers. Start asking them today. Ask them in-store, ask them by email, and make phone calls if you have to.

Secondly find out why they chose you. Was it price (tip: it often is NOT price) was it just because you were close, they saw your sign; a friend told them etc - another million reasons.

Deadly Sin No 8?

Deadly Sin No 8?

We're getting close to the end of part one now. Have you got any ideas what deadly sin number eight may be? I wonder if anybody hits on this.

The 8th Deadly Sin is: **Not Measuring Your Advertising Results.**

Someone once said, "Half my advertising works, I just don't know which half." I think it was Henry Ford of The Ford Motor Company. At the time was spending a fortune in advertising his motor cars.

If you don't measure your advertising then how on earth do you know if you're throwing money down the drain? I once asked an estate agent how much business they got from advertising in the local newspaper and he told me that he "didn't have a clue".

Here he was, a business established for decades that had advertised week in week out in a local paper for years and didn't know if it was working or not. He said "Truthfully, I don't think we get much from it" When I asked why he did it if it generated nothing he said to me "it's expected"

How much money was he spending? Three figures a week forever! How can you do that and not know if it's working? It may have been his best ever marketing channel or it may prove to be worthless. One thing I can guarantee is that when you do find out there will be quite a few surprises in store for you.

These days it's relatively easy to measure your advertising.

Firstly there's what's called 'telephone tracking numbers'. That's where you can have individual phone numbers, for individual advertisements. There are lots of companies; some of them sell bundles of tracking numbers with a local dialling code. You end up with ten different telephone numbers that you can put on each advertisement that you're running.

Yes there is a cost involved but I have to say that it's nowhere near the cost to you of not measuring your advertising

With your tracking numbers you will have access to a website where you can see how many calls that number generated how long you were on with them and any that were missed. Some are so advanced that when you pick up the phone they will 'whisper' where the call originated - How good is that! Anyone advertising in print that does not use tracking numbers is simply nuts.

If you do not use a telephone then you can use voucher codes. I'm sure you have seen this; you have a little number printed in the bottom corner as a reference that the reader quotes to you for your offer. That number relates to the magazine or place that you are actually advertising. Then there are coupon offers that people cut out and bring to you. Have a different offer in each publication or make sure there is a code on each different one.

Just so you know by the way, advertising sales people hate tracking numbers with a vengeance, they like advertising that is not tracked so they can say "well, you know advertising takes time to work, you never know how well it's really working" With tracking numbers it makes them answerable.
One area in which tracking numbers do struggle by the way is Radio as people cannot remember phone numbers from commercials. But there is still a way to measure radio *providing that you are measuring your other forms of advertising too!* If you want to know how to do that then it will be in a future book or you can email me and I'll explain.

Here's a thing, forget asking your customers where they heard of you or where they saw your offer. If you are marketing all the time then they just don't know where they heard of you and they'll search their brains for an answer that possibly is not true just to answer your question...

Many business owners think "well I ask all my customers where they heard of us" and I can tell you that that method simply does not work. Let me give you an example:

The TV that's sat in your lounge, what make is it? Let's say, for example, it's a Sony. If I said to you, "Why did you buy a Sony" Do you really know? You see Sony on street signs, you see Sony on the TV, and you see adverts in magazines, all over the place. You don't really know which specific 'touch point' made you decide Sony.

You probably looked on the net. You probably did searches for performance to find out what other people thought of them. Your friend may have one. There are myriad different reasons that lead you to Sony in the first place (or rather in the last place) before you actually decided to buy. So it's imperative that you measure where those leads are coming from when you do get them. Today, you need hard proven techniques for seeing where your money is well spent.

Action: as usual have a look at lots of advertisements. Notice the ones that do have voucher codes or different tracking numbers in different publications. You can bet that the ones who are using them are savvy marketers!

Part Two - How to Avoid The Deadly Sins

So, those are the deadly sins of advertising. There are many more than eight of course but get these primary ones right and your advertising will start to pay.

The second part of the book is learning how to avoid them; after all what would be the point of showing you those big mistakes without giving you an 'out'.

Before I take you through this step by step process I suggest you put down this book and go look at, listen to and watch some commercials. Watch the TV and see how many commercials have no call to action, how many are all me, me, me. Look how the major companies do it right but don't for one moment think they are immune. Major corporations are swayed by marketing designers that think their arty farty ideas are more important than the message.

Have a look at your local newspaper and you'll see all of these mistakes in local business advertising – too much content, me,me,me and all the others. Learn to identify those mistakes as an expert. After a while they will jump out at you.

What we do in part two is show you how to avoid these mistakes by the use of what we call an "advertising brief." Pulling one of those together and pulling a brand together is the next step in your journey.

Solution - The Brief

The solution to the deadly sins is all about what we call the advertising brief. Anyone worth their salt that sells you advertising will take a brief. By far the best way to choose your advertising is for you to do your brief yourself.

Too many small business owners pass on the responsibility for their advertising to the sales rep. They rely on advice from someone who quite possibly was previously selling blinds and curtains or double glazing. In most cases even they know more than the average business owner but they won't know more than you and that gives you power.

It gives you power to know whether the marketing channel they are offering will work for you and you will know exactly what criteria they have to meet to gain you as a client.

What I want you to do now is get yourself several sheets of paper and grab yourself a pen, because we are going to do this as we go through. Implementation is the key here.

Get your first sheet and on side one at the very top write "B**randing"**, and split the page in to three sections with lines that go from left to right; You can make them equal it's fine.

On side two, at the top, write **"Response"** and again, split the page into three sections with lines from left to right.

The next two pages are examples of what they will look like.

Don't skip this!

Side 1

Branding

Side 2

Response

Branding - Three Magic Words

There are two types of advertising and I briefly touched on this in part one. Those two types are *Branding* and *Response.* Branding is all about your company; response is something different that we'll come on to soon.

Branding is all about your company image and branding is all about **three magic words**. There is no weird science or anything to do with branding. You don't have to employ graphic designers and marketing consultants and all the rest. You can do the basics yourself and if you want to later on as your business grows you can expand that brand.

Three magic words then.

The Magic Words are **"who," "where" and "what."** This is all you need to know to do with branding.

Magic Branding Word One

The first magic branding word: **Who** are you?

You are either a company or a product. In most cases it's your business name. In others it's the name of the product.

For example, if you are solicitors it could be "Brown and Jones, Solicitors"; if you're a cleaning company it could be "Cleaneazy Bog Cleaners". If however you're a company that manufactures a product to sell then it could be the product. For example, Proctor and Gamble make 'Persil' washing detergent - so their branding would centre on the product 'Persil' but it most cases it's the name of your business.

Action: write down in section one WHO you are – choose one only – the product name or the business name

Magic Branding Word Two

Branding magic word number two: **Where** can people buy?

Where do you want people to go to actually spend money, as a result of your advertising? You've got a few options here.

Physical Address, that's your place of business, where they actually walk in, spend money with you and away they go.

Telephone Number, if people can spend money with you or book an appointment with you over the phone then that's this one

Your Website. Or online store

What you have to do is prioritise these three. The place where people actually hand over money for your product is your priority. If they buy at your place of business then that's priority one if they buy on the phone (actually book a service or buy a product) then that's a priority one. And if they can spend money on your website with a credit card then that's a priority one too.

If however your website is for information only then that's a priority two, if your phone number is for enquiries then that is priority two and if you sell via a website but not at your place of business then that's a priority two. **Your number one priority should be where people actually buy your product or service**

The reason for prioritising your 'where' is that some of your advertising channels will be time limited like for example your 30 seconds on Radio or TV.

Most of the time people can easily find your secondary priorities from Google or from a phone book. Getting your priority channels into the brain is another thing.

In print advertising it's not so important because you've got lots of room you can put your address and your phone number and your website in there, but even in print you should always find one to major on and make bigger and more exposed than the rest. If your advert in print is small you must choose your priority only.

Action: Write down in section two your 'Where' and the priority

Magic Branding Word Three

The Third Magic Word for branding is **What** do you do?

This is called the strapline and we are going to work on this quite heavily. If you haven't got a strapline for your business you need one.

Your strapline should be one of four general things. It's either:

*What you do
*What you believe in
*What values you have   or
*What people will experience

Let's give you some examples

Single words work well for some; it's a string of single words, for example,

"Trustable, Reliable, Likeable."
"Fixed, Fast, First' - that would be good for a repair company, wouldn't it?
'Taxis, Minibus, Coaches," says exactly what's on the tin.
"Connect, Engage, Drive," is a real world one from a car dealership, in America.
"Snap, Crackle and Pop," from Rice Crispies.

Example number two: what we do? This is a way of your strapline saying exactly what your business does in a very, short way. It captures the essence of your business offering in one short strapline.

"Making bread like no other."
"Dominoes pizza – it's what we do,"
"Fixed first time, every time,"
"The REAL thing,"

"We repair what your husband fixed," that's a real one that I like from a carpentry company.

Example number three "the things that you believe in" – as a business.

"Making a real difference housing people in need," that was a local housing association.
"Sustainable solutions in the throw away world." Very green isn't it that?
"The best a man can get," - Gillette.
"Save money live better," that's from Wal-Mart.

So they're talking about things that underpin the company and the company's beliefs.

Example number four: what people will experience? – Either by using your company or using your products or service.

"Finger Lickin' Good." that's KFC.
"We'll make you JUMP for joy," from a company that does parachute jumps.
"Feel The Magic," that was a radio station.
"I'm Lovin' it," - MacDonalds.

So they're all examples of branding. As you see doesn't have to be rocket science; it doesn't matter about the colours; it doesn't matter about the fonts - not for a small business. What matters is that you have a brand and that you use that brand throughout everything that you do. On your business cards, on your van, on your order forms, in your shop, on your signs, everywhere that you can think of - on your carpet if you can afford it!

Action: Here's a good exercise to develop your brand. Get a notepad and you and your staff write on it as many single words that you can think of to do with your business, service or product. Just write them down and use brainstorming rules (no idea is silly) a flipchart is good for this.

Do this for 15 minutes maximum. You're not trying to come up with your strapline for these 15 minutes, just focus on single words that describe either what you do, what you believe in, what people experience and what values you have.

After that just take 20 minutes inside yourself. Stare at the words and think of straplines – write any down that come to mind and then share them between you. You'll have a strapline that you all like and agree on within half an hour – don't overcook this; your best ideas will be within that timeframe.

Action: Write down in section three your strapline

Branding: Summary

You now have your brand. You have your name **"Who"**, your priority **'Where'** and your **"What"**.

You'll need some kind of logo to go with it and decide your company colours but these three areas are the pivot of your branding. Get someone to design you a logo based on your brief. You can issue that to a graphic designer if you like. There are dozens of great designers on fiverr.com that you can call upon for peanuts or you can do it yourself.

It's a good idea at this point to write your company brand ethos down on paper – write down what you believe in and what standards matter to you. Are you environmentally friendly? Are you aiming to sell on low cost and high volume? Etc – all of this is great information for marketing people and graphic designers.

Action: Write yourself in no more than two paragraphs your 'mission' statement. And then spend a maximum of two more paragraphs explaining how you will deliver that mission. Do it now, straight after your strapline brainstorm whilst all those words and values are fresh in your mind.

Response: Three More Magic Words

Now turn the paper over.

Putting together your response side will take longer than the branding so be prepared for a good session here.

We now move on to what we call **"Response"** advertising. And again, let me just cover what that is for you. Branding works but it works over time, it's the bit that people remember when they are thinking that they want your products or service and your name pops to mind; that's what branding is.

Response, however, is a different kind of advertising that includes *a call to action* and makes people want to buy what you have *now*. The best advertising campaigns of all have both branding *and* response.

Again we've got **Three Magic Words.** And they are **"What "Who," and "Why.".**

Response Magic Word One

The first magic word in response advertising is **What** are we selling?

Make a list on a separate piece of paper of all the services or products that you have for sale that you want to promote in the next six to twelve months. Take your time doing this.

Once complete I want you to choose just one product or service; only one. Now I know you're saying, "Oh how can I do that, I sell a million things" or "We have seven different services that we want to promote," If you're doing a marketing campaign you need to focus; remember part one? **One product: for One target: for One reason.** This is the process we use to choose that product or service. Save the rest on your sheet for your future campaigns but for now just choose one.

Action: write down in section one **What** you are going to promote with this campaign

Response Magic Word Two

The second magic word with response advertising is **"Who"**. More specifically it's **who** are we selling to? Our target prospect.

Make a list on another piece of paper of every target that would want your product or service. Start with what you can do with your product then ask yourself what the typical prospect for that application is like. Are they male or female? How old are they? Are they married? single?, straight or gay? Do they have children? What do they do with your product? It's fine if they are all those things of course but in most cases you can drill down into your target. The harder you drill down the easier it is to find somewhere suitable to advertise to them.

Obviously your answers will be determined by your knowledge of your product. If you say "everyone needs my product" then you are very mistaken and must really drill down on your target. An example - if you're selling paving slabs, who is your target customer right now? Is it the jobbing builder, is it the DIY man, and is it a DJ (seriously! They put slabs under record decks!)

When complete, look at your list and knowing what you know about your product / service ask the question "Which one will make me the most money right now?"

Action: Write down in section two **Who** we want to influence to buy our product / service and describe them in detail. In effect you paint a picture of your target prospect in words, because if you don't know who your target is, how do you know where they are going to be? How do you know which medium to choose?

Response Magic Word Three

Magic word number three then is **"Why"** Why would they buy from you, and more importantly why will they buy from you *now*?

List on a separate piece of paper every compelling reason that they would want to buy your product or service..

This part of the process is where you will craft your 'compelling reason' for them to do business with you. Think this through from their perspective; put yourself in their shoes. What can you offer them that would compel them to buy from you today?

When you're thinking about putting an offer together you could be thinking, "Well we will offer a discount." **A good offer should not cost you money, it should make you money**; always remember that. Rather than doing a '30% off sale' take a second look. If they're buying paving slabs you could do an offer that says, "Buy ten slabs and get a 10kg bag of sand free. Buy ten more get another bag of sand free!" That is so much better than giving money off, and it works better because it's a perceived added value.

Buyers like to receive something more than they initially wanted if it means they will save money or time. So what can you offer them? What do they need to do with your product or service, and why will they buy from you rather than Joe down the road? There might be a million reasons. You'll probably think to yourself, "Well it's price I'm cheaper than him," that may be true, but it also may be that they know of your experience; they trust you; or you're hundred yards away from where they live - so you're close.

If you don't know why people buy from you, ask them. "Why did you choose to buy this from us today, when there are twenty more suppliers within a ten mile radius?" Find out why, because those are the things that people buy for; and very often it is not the reasons that you think.

Get it down to one compelling reason; remember the campaign is going to be one product; to one target; for one reason.

Let me illustrate the point with a personal story.

My wife of 30 years religiously goes to the hairdresser every Saturday. It's almost a ritual with her. She loves her 'bling' and loves to feel good about herself. Having her hair and nails done is all it takes so who am I to argue?

Anyway, last Saturday was 'colour week' – around every four to five weeks she has a colour applied and it's a good 90 minute job (the ladies reading this will be well aware)

The salon she uses is a quite high end one for our area. It's clean, well managed and they are ALWAYS upselling the services they provide. Many think that they are expensive but in truth although it *feels* expensive they are only a few more pounds than the competition.

The place is super clean, has good signage and it feels like it's a place to be pampered. Upon entering the salon her coat is taken by someone on reception and hung up carefully and they make her a really nice cappuccino (I know as I've had one too) this all adds to the feeling that she is in a quality salon.

Last Saturday she came to the car with a small box in her hand. She looked at me with a beaming smile and asked "do you like my hair?" As usual I complemented her on the look and said she looked great. She was genuinely excited this time though, although the overall effect was just as good every week **she felt more special** this week.

"I've had a free treatment" she said "It feels really silky and smooth today – They put this stuff on my hair" At this point she revealed a glossy box with a spray in it. "Bet that was expensive" I replied, just like most men; "No! She said, because I had a free treatment with it **and I saved two pounds on the bottle!**"

The bottle of spray was a branded one from a company called GHD – again ladies will recognise that brand as one of the best in straighteners, dryers and tongs. They've now branched out into hair care products too.

"The bottle was usually seventeen pounds, but I got two pounds off and they gave me a free treatment" To her the two pounds off and the free treatment was a bargain to be had. Think about that… **just two pounds to make a customer happy.**

The two pounds reduction also distracted her mind from the price of the first item that she had paid for - her colour.

What a great upsell offer that was. For the sake of £2 and probably 10p's worth of their own bottle they made an offer that many find irresistible. The client got a good deal, bought something they would not have known about, felt a million dollars and the salon increased the sale from that client by £15 – that's about 20% more than she would normally spend.

Now that's a good offer – **It made the salon money and didn't cost them money**.

The short-sighted salon owner would say they had lost money because they didn't get the correct retail price of the product. What they miss out on is that the sale would never have taken place without the offer. Even if the bottle cost price was £10 it was more profit in the tills.

What are people using the product in section one for that has a complementary product that they don't normally buy? What else can you sell them?

The next thing to add to your compelling reason is some scarcity. We not only have to make them an offer - we have to compel them to buy NOW.

Direct sales people are very good at this where their product is sold in one visit. They know that if they leave the house or business without an order they are much less likely to get the order.

They will always have an offer that runs out today. A cancellation that needs to be filled, a company offer that ends today, an offer from last week that he can squeeze in for you. I'm sure you've experienced this yourself.

To compel someone to buy you have to pull together a really good offer, and then make that offer limited in some way. "Ends this month" "Only 25 available at this price" etc

This is often hard for small business owners. "I don't want to do it this way, it feels wrong" they tell me. It's not wrong, it's your business and if you want to make an offer then that's your business!

What's wrong with that???

If you don't make some sort of offer then you shouldn't be considering advertising. It's like a toothless tiger without one.

Make your offer real, believable and scarce.

Action: write in section three your compelling reason for people to buy now.

You are now ready to put your campaign together.

The Brief: Summary

You now have your branding, you know what you want people to think about your business, its values and you can clearly identify where you want to send them to buy. Your business name and strapline combined make it clear who you are and what you do. Your branding is transferable to any kind of advertising that you do and on everything you produce that is seen by the public. You only have to design your brand once and then transfer it to every campaign you ever run.

You also have your first response campaign brief. You know exactly who you are aiming at, what you want them to buy and why they will buy it. You will make many response campaigns throughout your business life. The method taught in this book of how to craft that campaign is the same every time – three magic words.

You also have several ideas for subsequent campaigns as you have notes of other targets and why they will buy. You have your compelling reason that will make them want to buy rather than you have to sell. People love to buy but hate to be sold.

Do as many response briefs as you have targets. Choose your best three of four and you have the beginnings of a campaign.

A Campaign remembers is a series of advertisements for the same product the different targets for different reasons.

Next Steps

The next steps that you have to make in your campaigns are:

"Where should I advertise?"
"How can I leverage that advertising?"
"How should I advertise?"

With the brief in hand you can find out where to advertise – where does your target read, listen or watch? You know who they are so why not ask them? What newspapers do they read/ what radio stations and which programmes do they listen to?

When your advertising rep calls you now have the upper hand, the power is with you. Do not tell them who you need to reach - ask them to tell you who reads, listens or watches their publication, station or channel. Make them tell you what the demographic is and make them prove it. If that demographic matches your brief then you might be a buyer. If it does not match then what's the point of buying advertising? *The fish you have bait for are not in that lake*

From here on in it is all about creativity. Look what your competitors are doing, look what the national companies in your niche are doing – see what works. Find original ways of getting your compelling reason out there and co-ordinate your 'campaign'

The rest of your journey in advertising is for another book. I could write a whole book just about how to advertise on the radio (and I probably will) along with another talking about newspapers.

This book was all about avoiding the common mistakes - The 8 Deadly Sins of Advertising. Together we have identified them and I dare say that you've learned a lot. You know how to write yourself a brief and how to avoid those glaring mistakes that so many others make.

From here on in you can look at your advertising with new eyes. You have knowledge and ammunition when the sales rep comes calling and you know the questions to ask about demographics and coverage.

The mind of the media sales rep is all about one thing - "How can I make money from this business" Don't be quick to tell him what you need, keep that information for yourself. Make them work for it by giving you the information you need. You are in control now.

Reps often spout numbers. A newspaper rep will tell you that for every copy sold they have 2.2 readers. A radio station rep may tell you that they have a 'potential' X listeners. You don't want potential, you want actual numbers.

The number of listeners or readers doesn't matter nearly as much as the demographic. As a smart marketer you don't need numbers so much as you need quality targets. I would sooner advertise to 1000 highly targeted readers that I know will respond to my offer than 20,000 of the general population. It's cheaper and more effective.

Final Notes

That's your lot then. I believe that I have delivered on my promise to you but if not then do let me know how it could be improved. I really hope that you have found this book useful.

If you have enjoyed the book, can I ask that you leave me a positive review on Amazon. I read every review personally.

I'm occasionally convinced to help out as a consultant. If you'd like to talk to me about this then drop me an email to glyn@marketingformugs.com

Finally you can learn even more by joining my email list at http://marketingformugs.com

Keep Marketing!

About The Author

Glyn's background in sales started in his late twenties when he became disillusioned with the engineering work that he had 'served his time' in. In fact, during a period of two years during the manufacturing decline in the 1980's he was made redundant three times in businesses that were failing.

The whole engineering industry was suffering, what with union action and a recession where the rich got very wealthy and those who provided the raw materials for the wealth were squeezed by cheap foreign labour and imports.

Glyn wanted more and looked to self employment. The first step was, believe it or not, a window cleaning business. Now this you would think may not be a real 'Sales & Marketing' kind of role but building a list of 200 customers involved time walking the streets of Derbyshire **knocking on doors,** learning all about referrals and of course customer retention and expectations. Isn't that what we all have to do?

From a very young age Glyn had ambitions to be in the radio business and as a 'DJ' at the weekend he would leave the 'shammy' in the bucket and perform in front of often hundreds of people, young and old, as he built a **disco business**. This was extra money and soon he found himself making more than the average wage through the two sources of income.

In 1993 Glyn learned of a new initiative from the UK Government for a thing called 'Community Radio' and set about to find more information. He approached influential people in his area to leverage their influence in a bid to be one of the first to trial this new media.

His Local MP Phillip Oppenheim was persuaded that helping Glyn was a good thing to do and rallied around the Houses of Parliament to help in this quest.

Glyn used publicity in local newspapers and leaflets to get together many like minded people who wanted to be involved. The Valley Radio Group was born.

He approached local business leaders to help fund this venture and attracted the likes of Thorntons Chocolates, Trent Buses and many others by enthusing corporate directors with his idea of a real local service.

In 1994 Glyn opened the microphone for the very first time on the medium wave band of 1386Khz and began a 28 day trial 'Restricted Service Licence'.

Glyn was not the first to take advantage of the licence offering but was the 9th person in the whole of the UK to do so.

Glyn had to become very marketing savvy in a short time, selling advertising on the station, creating the messages and commercials and learning the ropes of how to get paid and run a professional business.

Three more 28 day licences came and went over a two year period, each one of them better than the last and more and more profitable. The whole idea of this activity was with the express intention of gaining a full licence to serve his community 24 hours a day.

Alas this was not to be. The radio authority made no moves to offer this despite an overwhelming reaction from the public at large. In 1996 Glyn decided that without a full licence in the offering he would not return to the airwaves and that there was little point. Lessons learned from this were to be invaluable in the future.

Glyn returned to education and took a City & Guilds in computer engineering working on database design and automation techniques. At this time the most powerful computer was called a '386' and his first 1 GB hard drive cost a small fortune.

He landed a position with Rolls-Royce Aerospace in Derby looking developing a parts tracking database on a marine development project for the US Navy.

During this position he found an internal advertisement for a communications manager inside a 'change management' team that were implementing new ways for the global monolith to do business. He got the job inside 'BPF' (Better performance faster) and went on to champion internal and external communications for the initiative and supply chain.

What he found surprised him, he found that he had a skill that the big guns did not possess. The ability to dissect complicated ideas into plain English so that the general workforce of the company could understand complicated issues.

He directed the people at the very top of the organisation in video communications, advised engineers how to structure their messages when disseminating their messages through to the supply chain. As this was second nature to Glyn from his radio days he laughed that this was so valued by people earning hundreds of thousands more than him.

When the improvement program came to a successful end, Glyn decided to move into direct sales and here the real variety began. He sold door to door Gas and Electricity contracts for a major company Powergen. He sold business insurance for an American company.

Then moved onto domestic home improvements with Windows, Conservatories and Kitchens.

One day whilst with a client he was sat giving the 'sales pitch' when the guy he was speaking to got a phone call – during that five minute call the guy made over three thousand pounds!. It turned out the guy was a middle man supplying finance to people with poor credit histories and generated his business with a simple two inch square advertisement in 'Exchange and Mart' a motor sales magazine.

Glyn had learned that the quality of your life is determined by the questions you ask yourself. So he sat down and asked himself "How can I make more money without even leaving home or taking off my pyjamas"

The answer came swift "sell something" – it's the fastest way to riches – but sell what and where? "Sell on the Internet" was the reply to the question.

Glyn's first internet company was born and armed with his computer knowledge Glyn wrote e-books, designed software and sold CD's of freeware on eBay and through 17 different websites. The business grew to a point where his wife joined the business as 'chief mailer'

One customer who bought an e-book from Glyn used the username 'daytrader_pitbull' on eBay and was destined to push Glyn in a new direction.

Having heard the phrase 'Day Trader' on a recent Panorama BBC TV programme, Glyn engaged in a conversation that would lead him into the world of Foreign exchange currency Speculation. He ended up trading full time for several years, made significant amounts of money, still trades to this day and is a respected source of advice and information for upcoming traders.

Despite this success the market crash of 2008 left him scarred and Glyn needed a reason to stay away from the markets. An old school friend that Glyn introduced to the world of radio all those years ago had finally got a licence for a 'community' radio station and needed someone to head up the sales.

After asking for many months, and with the intention of staying for only a year to put procedures in place, Glyn accepted the offer. He was still there four years later and had managed over £700,000 in sales for a small town station.

In January 2011 Glyn had an operation for 'High Grade Dysphonia' which is about as close to cancer as you can get. It was on his vocal chords and involved two sessions of laser surgery four months apart to remove the offending cells. Suddenly he could no longer be a radio personality (something he had carried on for many years) and face to face or telephone sales were impossible during the healing process.

As this book is published it's just over a year since that operation and the voice is returning slowly. In early 2013 the radio station ended the contract as Glyn could no longer sell with the same impact as he did before.

This is his first business book and the first in his new business. Without a voice what do you do to give people the information you have? You write.

Welcome to the next chapter in Glyn's life.

If you enjoyed this book and found it useful, please leave a positive review on amazon to tell others that it may help them too!

Book Link On Amazon

Join the mailing list at marketingformugs.com for more great tips on marketing your business

www.ingramcontent.com/pod-product-compliance
Lightning Source LLC
Chambersburg PA
CBHW071646170526
45166CB00003B/1451